To order additional copies of this book, contact
Partridge India
000 800 10062 62
www.partridgepublishing.com/india
orders.india@partridgepublishing.com

04/18/2017

PARTRIDGE

AN INTRODUCTION TO COMPUTERS

Volume One

Nwaiwu Ifeanyi Princewill

Chapter - 1

My Desktop Computer

Lesson – 1.1: What is a Computer?

Take a look at the computer in front of you. No, not just the screen. Look at all of the other parts. Do you know what they are? Do you know what they do? If you already know - great! Give yourself a big pat on the back! But if you don't know about all the gadgets surrounding your computer, then read on and find out!

⊕ A computer is an electronic machine.

⊕ A computer is an electronic machine that inputs, process, outputs and stores data.

Lesson - 1.2:
DIFFERENCE BETWEEN **TELEVISION** AND **COMPUTER**.

TELEVISION

➢ It has no keyboard, mouse, printer and others.

➢ It only has Video or DVD machine.

COMPUTER

It has all the parts of the computer like a keyboard, mouse, printer and others.

Parts of the Body

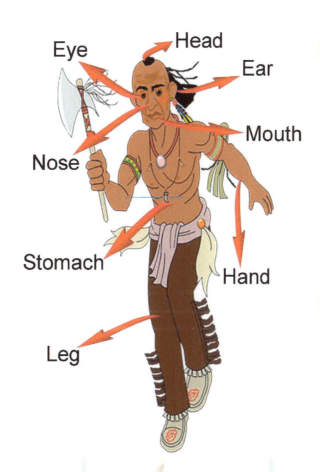

Lesson – 1.3: PARTS OF A DESKTOP COMPUTER

The same way we have parts of the body is the same way a computer has parts. The basic parts of a desktop computer are system unit, monitor, keyboard, and mouse. Each part plays an important role whenever you use a computer.

1. Monitor

2. Mouse

3. Microphone

4. Modem

5. System Unit

6. Speaker

7. Scanner

8. Printer

9. Keyboard

Singing Time

Twinkle, twinkle, little star,
How I wonder what you are.
Up above the world so high,
Like a diamond in the sky.
Twinkle, twinkle, little star,
How I wonder what you are.

4M….3S……P…...K
4M….3S……P…...K
4M….3S……P…...K
These are the parts of Computer
These are the parts of Computer
These are the parts of Computer

MY BODY	COMPUTER	MY BODY	COMPUTER

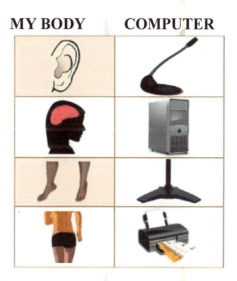

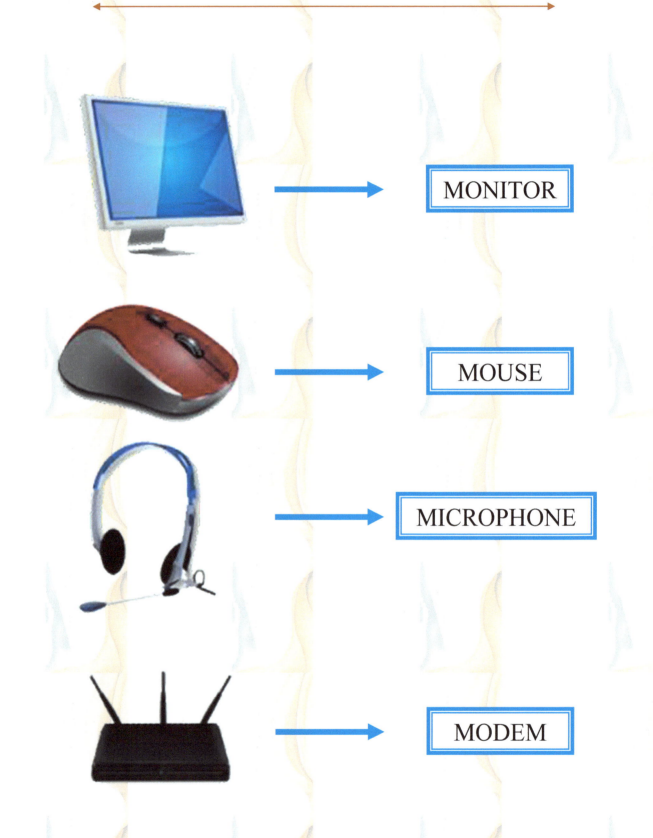

MONITOR

MOUSE

MICROPHONE

MODEM

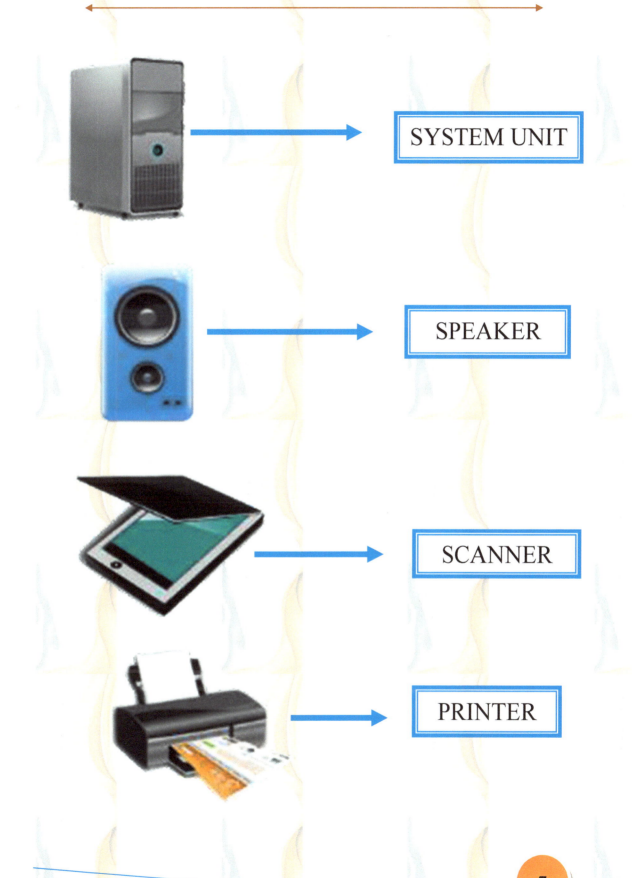

SYSTEM UNIT

SPEAKER

SCANNER

PRINTER

KEYBOARD

Quick-Check (1)

Circle the pictures that represent a computer.

$$\overline{12}$$

Quick-Check (2)

$$\overline{12}$$

Choose the correct word to complete the sentence

(1.)   Computer is an electronic _____.

      a. water
      b. machine
      c. monitor

Spelling Time

Complete the following words with the correct letter(s).

c	u	r	n	i

(1.)   Comp__ter

(2.)   Elect__on__c

(3.)   Ma__hi__e

Quick-Check (3)

$\overline{8}$

Write the name of each computer part below.

 ⟶ A.) ....

 ⟶ B.) ....

 ⟶ C.) ....

 ⟶ D.) ....

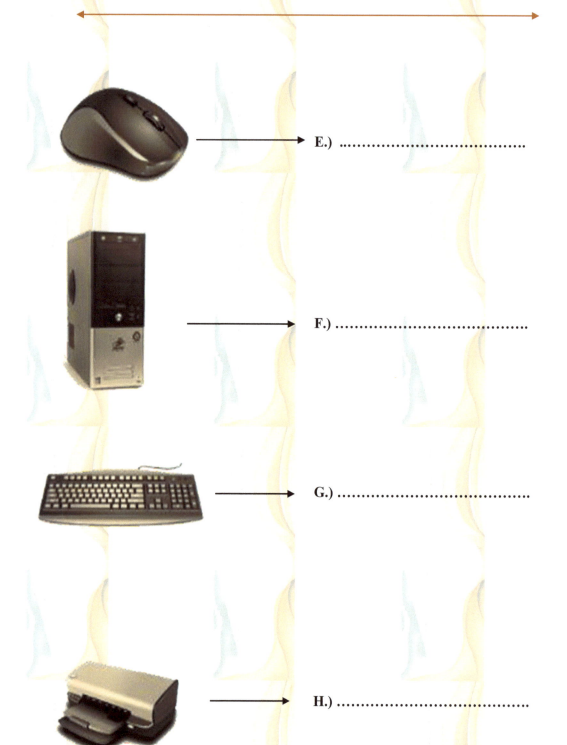

E.) ....

F.) ....

G.) ....

H.) ....

Quick-Check (4)

James is confused; he could not find the parts of his desktop computer in his room.

What information about James is given?

Circle the information given in the picture above.
An example has been given to you.

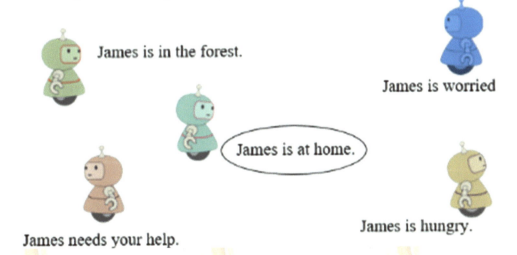

Quick-Check (5)

Draw a line to match each technology tool to its use.

5

- Used to send and receive information from one computer to another.

- Used to point and click on an object on screen.

- Used to print work on paper or hardcopy.

- Used to capture images such as magazine pages, into computer.

- Used to show data that has been put in a computer.

Quick-Check (6)

Rank: _____

Find the computers!

How many computers are there in the picture below?
.

Answer: _____

Chapter - 2

My Computer Monitor

Lesson – 2.1: What is a Monitor?

- **A monitor** is the computer screen.

Monitor displays picture on the screen.

Lesson – 2.2: Two Types of Monitors

1.) **Colour** Monitor.

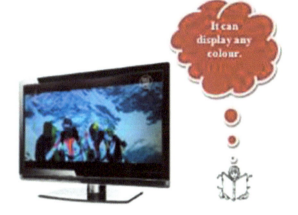

2.) **Monochrome** Monitor.

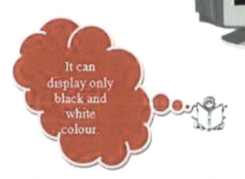

Lesson – 2.3: External Parts of the Monitor

The external parts of a monitor are those parts that make a device a monitor. In this lesson we will study the parts that make up a monitor.

1.   Screen

3.   Power Switch

2.   Casing

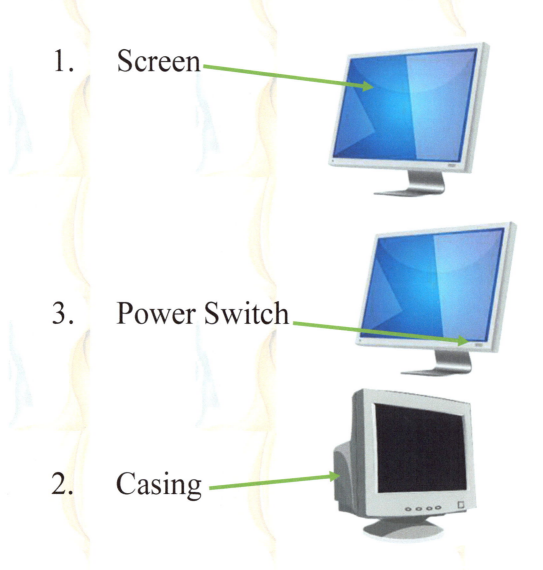

4. Monitor Stand

5. Monitor Cable

6. Power Cable

Rank: _____

Colour the pictures with a suitable colour(s).

2. Coloured Monitor.

- It has all the colours.

1. Monochrome Monitor.

- It has only black and white colours.

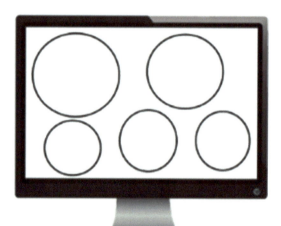

Quick-Check (8)

Label the parts of the Monitor

6

(Power Switch, Casing, Screen, Stand, Power Cable, Monitor Cable)

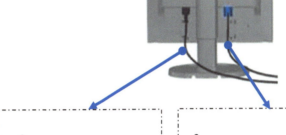

1. _____

2. _____
   _____

3. _____
   _____

4. _____

5. _____
   _____

6. _____
   _____

INTRODUCTION TO COMPUTER-1 (Starter)

Quick-Check (9)

9

 **Chapter - 3**

My Computer Mouse

Lesson – 3.1: What is a Computer Mouse?

➢ A **mouse** is used to click or select object on the screen.

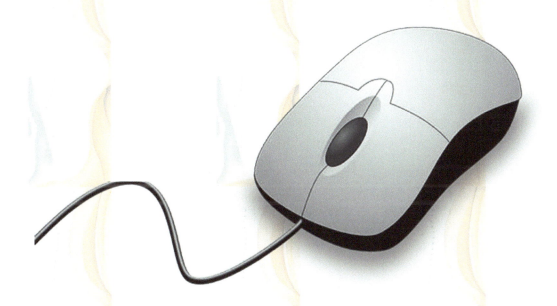

Lesson – 3.2: Three Types of Computer Mouse

1.)   Traditional Mouse.

> It has a long cable and a track ball.

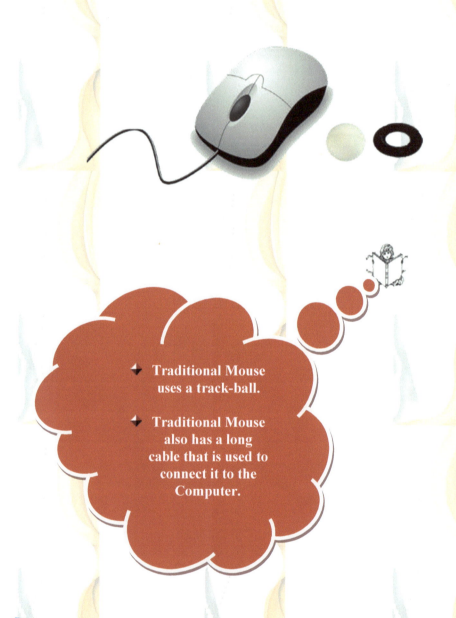

✦ Traditional Mouse uses a track-ball.

✦ Traditional Mouse also has a long cable that is used to connect it to the Computer.

2.)   Optical Mouse.

➢ It has long cable, Light Emitting Diode and a sensor.

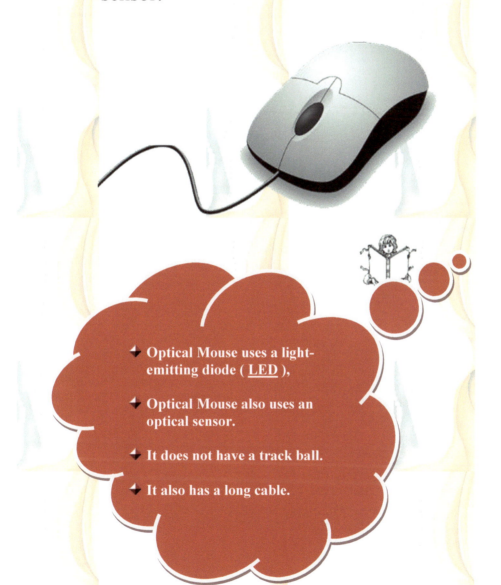

+ **Optical Mouse uses a light-emitting diode (LED),**

+ **Optical Mouse also uses an optical sensor.**

+ **It does not have a track ball.**

+ **It also has a long cable.**

3.) Optical Wireless Mouse.

➢ It has no long cable.

➢ It uses a program to connect with the computer.

✦ Optical wireless Mouse uses Infra-Red or Blue Tooth to connect.

✦ It can be used from a far distance.

✦ It has no track ball.

Lesson – 3.3: Differences between Traditional, Optical and Optical Wireless Mouse

S/N	PARTS	TRADITIONAL MOUSE	OPTICAL MOUSE	OPTICAL WIRELESS MOUSE
1.	Long cable	Yes	Yes	No
2.	Sensor	No	Yes	Yes
3.	Light Emitting Diode	No	Yes	Yes
4.	Track Ball	Yes	No	No
5.	USB Connector	No	No	Yes
6.	Scroll Wheel	No	Yes	Yes

Lesson – 3.4: Parts of a Computer-mouse

2. Buttons

1. Long-Cable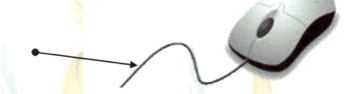

3. Palm-Rest

4. Track-Ball

5. USB-Connector

6. Scroll-Wheel

Front Side of the Mouse

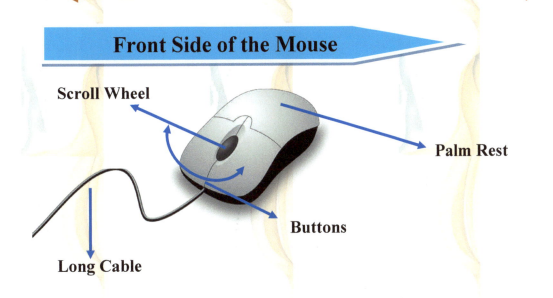

Scroll Wheel

Palm Rest

Long Cable

Buttons

Back Side of the Mouse

Track Ball

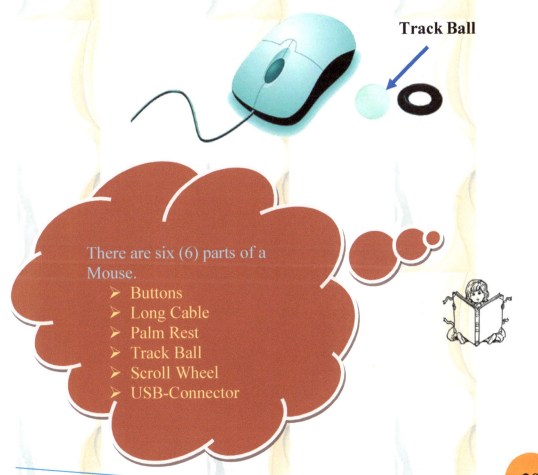

There are six (6) parts of a Mouse.
- ➢ Buttons
- ➢ Long Cable
- ➢ Palm Rest
- ➢ Track Ball
- ➢ Scroll Wheel
- ➢ USB-Connector

Other

USB Connector

Two Types of Buttons

Left Button

Right Button

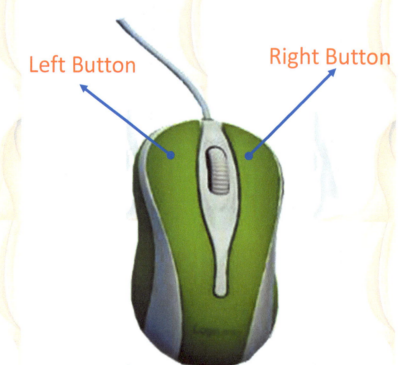

1. RIGHT BUTTON:

- We depress the right-button once.
- It is used to choose options like copy, paste, refresh, new, etc.

2. LEFT BUTTON:

- We depress this button twice or once and it is used to select object on the screen.

Lesson – 3.5: Functions of Mouse

➢ **There are four functions of the Mouse, they are;**

1. Dragging

Press the left button and move to the right, left, up or down.

2. Click

Depress the button once.

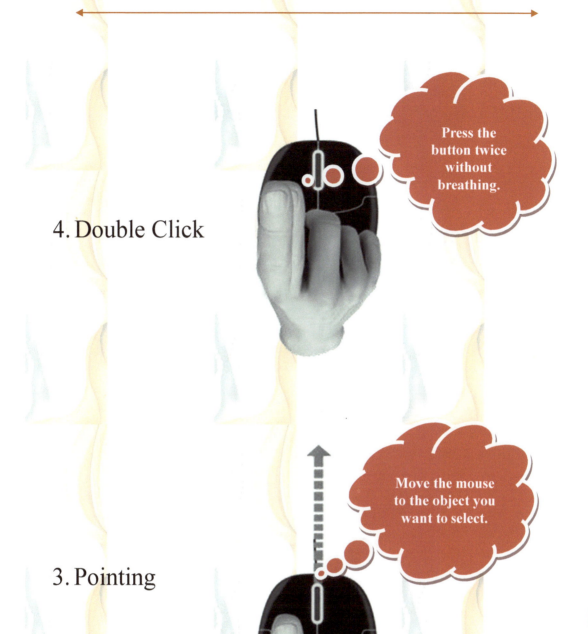

4. Double Click

Press the button twice without breathing.

3. Pointing

Move the mouse to the object you want to select.

Lesson – 3.6: Two types of Click

1. Right Click

Press the right button.

Press the left button.

2. Left Click

PRACTICAL

ONLINE EXERCISE ON HOW TO USE THE MOUSE

Type the web address below on your Internet Address bar

Visit :→

http://www.seniornet.org/howto/mouseexercises/mousepractice.html

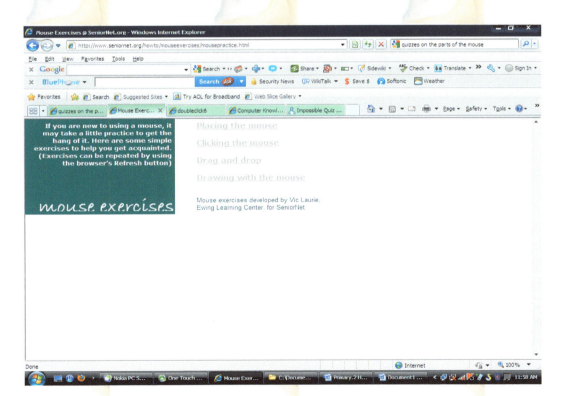

INTRODUCTION TO COMPUTER-1 (Starter)

PUZZLE GAME ON FUNCTIONS, TYPES AND PARTS OF THE MOUSE

INSTRUCTION: You have to trace these words both **verticals** (↓) and **horizontals** (→) and colour each word; (Optical Mouse, Traditional Mouse, Optical Wireless, Long Cable, Buttons, Palm Rest, Track Ball, Pointing, Clicking, Double Clicking, Dragging, Left, Right)

NOTE: Each word is connected to another

O	P	T	I	C	A	L	C	M	O	U	S	E	A	B	D	E	F
W	E	R	L	C	O	O	M	E	W	D	D	G	H	I	A	J	K
T	H	A	F	L	Z	N	P	W	V	W	O	L	M	N	N	O	P
E	O	D	R	A	G	G	I	N	G	A	U	Q	R	S	G	T	U
L	U	I	F	Z	Y	Q	T	B	W	E	B	S	I	T	E	Y	F
E	S	T	E	Z	X	C	E	I	O	R	L	E	F	T	R	E	I
V	E	I	L	Y	P	A	L	M	R	R	E	S	T	R	I	L	L
I	K	O	L	B	O	B	R	S	L	I	P	M	R	I	G	H	T
S	E	N	O	O	I	L	P	C	D	N	C	A	A	K	O	L	M
I	E	A	W	Y	N	E	R	U	C	G	L	R	C	E	U	O	O
O	P	L	S	R	T	E	I	I	U	E	I	R	K	U	S	W	L
N	E	T	C	L	I	C	K	I	N	G	C	I	D	P	B	C	A
R	R	M	I	Q	N	O	N	T	P	G	K	A	B	S	A	L	S
A	Q	O	P	O	G	C	C	G	L	S	I	G	A	K	G	U	K
D	B	U	T	T	O	N	S	K	A	N	N	G	L	A	F	R	O
I	V	S	K	O	X	V	T	R	U	C	G	K	L	I	A	N	G
O	W	E	H	A	T	I	T	T	A	K	E	S	T	O	N	B	E
S	R	O	A	D	M	A	Y	O	R	P	R	I	M	A	R	Y	I
O	P	T	I	C	A	L	L	W	I	R	E	L	E	S	S	K	J
E	N	C	Y	C	L	O	P	E	D	I	A	E	D	U	V	I	N

Quick-Check (10)

5

Fill in each blank with the correct answer.

(Palm-rest, Scroll-wheel, Long-cable, USB-connector, Buttons)

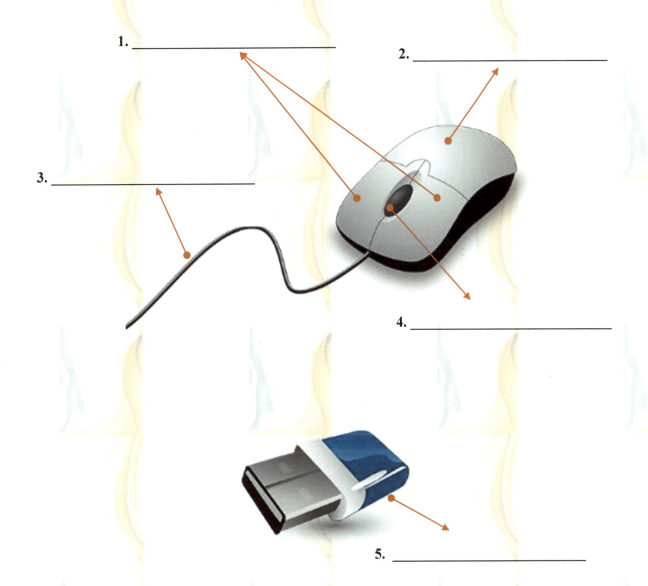

1. _____

2. _____

3. _____

4. _____

5. _____

Quick-Check (11)

Find the words!

$\overline{5}$

Six parts of a mouse are hidden in the puzzle.
The words may go across, down or diagonally.
Use the words given below to help you.
You can find an example below.

USB-CONNECTOR   PALM-REST   BUTTONS

LONG-CABLE   SCROLL-WHEEL   TRACK-BALL

U	M	B	R	E	L	L	A	M	O	N	K
A	S	E	A	N	R	I	C	E	U	P	S
A	B	B	U	T	T	O	N	S	L	I	E
P	E	A	C	O	C	K	S	L	O	L	Y
O	R	E	A	O	N	G	A	E	B	O	Y
A	S	E	R	N	N	B	L	A	G	I	R
B	A	R	Y	L	O	N	C	N	A	I	A
L	I	M	K	K	O	W	E	I	N	G	S
L	I	O	C	N	G	P	I	C	G	E	O
W	H	A	I	N	T	E	B	O	T	A	R
D	R	P	O	R	O	J	E	C	T	O	R
T	M	L	O	N	I	T	O	R	L	E	R

Quick-Check (12)

Choose the correct options in question to fill-in the blank space.

1) _____ is to press the left button and move to the right, left, up or down. ( )

    (a.) Click
    (b.) Double-click
    (c.) Dragging

2) _____ is to move the mouse to the object you want to select. ( )

    (a.) Dragging
    (b.) Pointing
    (c.) Dragging

3) _____ is to press the button once. ( )

    (a.) Click
    (b.) Pointing
    (c.) Double-click

4) _____ is to press the button twice without breathing. ( )

    (a.) Click
    (b.) Double-click
    (c.) Pointing

Chapter - 4

My System Unit

Most of today's computers are housed in towers. A tower is a vertical case that encloses the motherboard and all connected chip sets and drives that make up the computer.

Lesson – 4.1: What is a System Unit?

> A system unit is the brain of the computer because it tells a computer what to do.

System Unit is the brain of the computer.

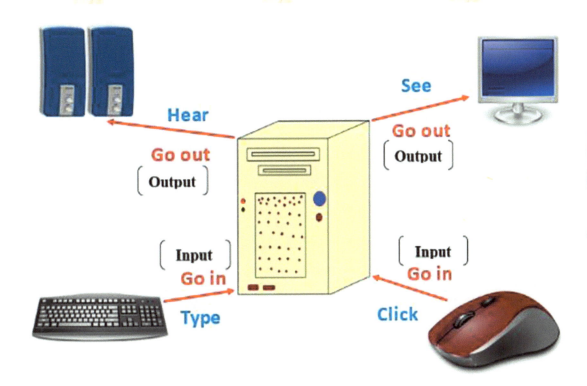

Lesson – 4.2: EXTERNAL PARTS OF THE SYSTEM UNIT

1.) Casing.	4.) Light Emitting Diode.
2.) Power Switch	5.) Thumb Drive.
3.) Reset Switch.	6.) DVD Drive.

1. Casing:

The power on/off switch is used to turn on or off the power to the Computer.

2. Power switch:

The power On/Off switch is used to turn on or off the power to the PC.

3. Reset switch:

This button helps you restart your computer without disconnecting the power supply.

4. Light Emitting Diode:

These lights are used to show whether the *hard disk, the floppy disk* or the **CD** is being read or written.

5. Thumb drive:

The thumb disk drive is used to read the information stored in flash drive or Thumb device.

6. DVD Drive:

DVD drive is a device that reads the information stored on DVD.

Lesson – 4.3: Diagram of the External Parts Of The System Unit

A computer system unit is the enclosure that contains the main components of a computer. It is also referred to as computer case or tower. Read on to learn about the external parts use in computer system unit.

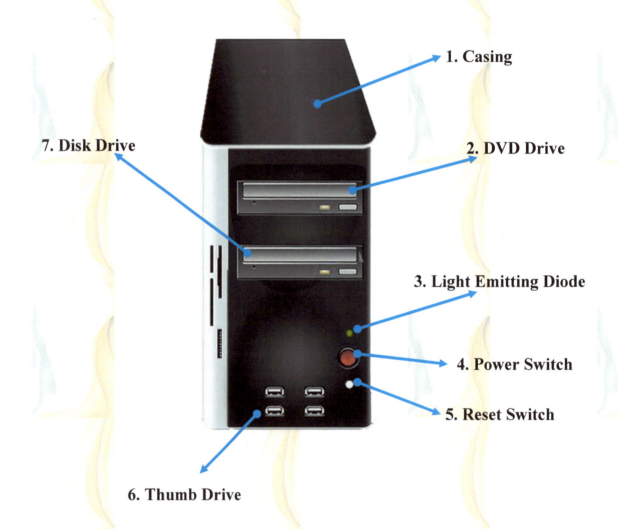

1. Casing

7. Disk Drive

2. DVD Drive

3. Light Emitting Diode

4. Power Switch

5. Reset Switch

6. Thumb Drive

Lesson – 4.4: **Uses of the System Unit**

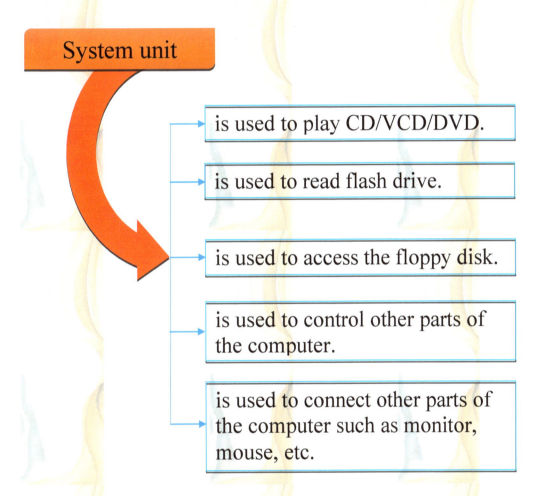

System unit

is used to play CD/VCD/DVD.

is used to read flash drive.

is used to access the floppy disk.

is used to control other parts of the computer.

is used to connect other parts of the computer such as monitor, mouse, etc.

Quick-Check (13)

7

PARTS OF A COMPUTER SYSTEM UNIT

The picture below shows the parts of a computer system unit. Fill in the lines with the appropriate names of the external parts of the system unit. An example has been given to you

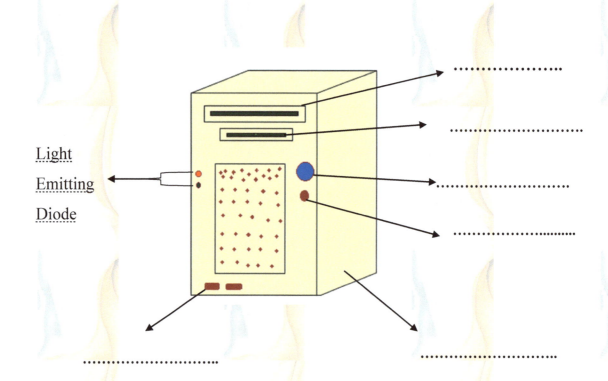

Light Emitting Diode

Quick-Check (14)

$\overline{4}$

FUNCTIONS OF THE SYSTEM UNIT

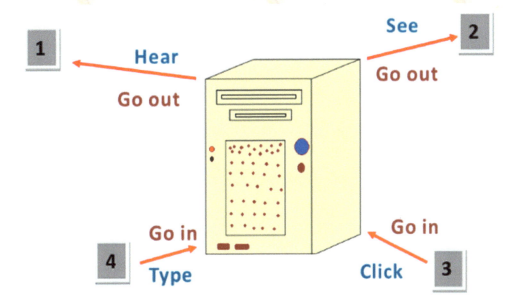

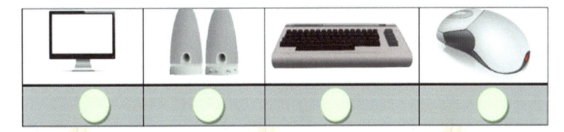

My Printer

➔ Here is the information about different types of printers you should know.

➔ The main categories are: - laser printers, ink-jets, dot-matrix, multifunctional, etc.

➔ Normally home computer users will use ink-jets as they are relatively cheap but superior in quality to dot-matrix.

➔ Laser jets and other printers created by new technology are more expensive and more commonly found in the offices.

○ Teacher Guide

Lesson – 5.1: What is a Printer?

➢ **A printer is used to print object on paper.**

Lesson – 5.2: Types of Printers?

There are three main types of printers:

1. Laser-jet Printer

✦ The laser printer is very expensive to buy but cheapest to run.

✦ The output quality is very high, and it prints very fast.

2. Ink-jet Printer

✦ These are cheap to buy.

✦ The quality of print is high, and they are quite fast printers.

✦ However, the printer inks are very expensive.

1. Dot matrix Printer

✦ It's very old, very slow, and very noisy.

✦ IT also has a poor output quality.

✦ However, it's cheap to buy and fairly reliable.

OTHER PRINTERS:
Multifunction Printer.

- It can print.

- It can copy.

- It can scan

- It can fax.

Quick-Check (15)

6

Choose the options in parenthesis to fill-in the blank spaces

1. _____ is used to print our work on paper.   (   )

    a. Monitor
    b. Scanner
    c. Printer

2. We have _____ types of printer.   (   )

    a. two
    b. three
    c. eight

3. Which picture shows a Printer?   (   )

a.

b.

c.

4. Which of the printer can scan, copy and print?   (   )

    a. Laser printer
    b. Multifunctional printer
    c. Ink-jet printer
    d. Dot matrix printer

5. Which of the printer is the fastest?   (   )

    a. Laser printer
    b. Ink-Jet printer
    c. Dot matrix printer

6. Which of the printer is the slowest?   (   )

    a. Laser printer
    b. Ink-Jet printer
    c. Dot matrix printer

Chapter – 6

My Computer Room

Lesson – 6.1: The Computer Room

2.) Remove your shoes before you enter your computer room.

1.) Never take any food like candies, chocolates, chewing gum inside the computer room.

3.)   Keep the computer room clean.

5.)   Shut the door of the computer-room properly.

4.)   Turn-off the computer properly after use.

Lesson -6.2: The Power Supply

1.) Turn on the switch at the source of the POWER SUPPLY.

4.) Turn on the UPS to regulate the flow of current.

2.) Turn on the POWER SWITCH of the Monitor.

4.) Turn on the SYSTEM UNIT.

Practical Time!

Exercise 1

Use the appraisal list below to grade the performance of the pupils in the following skills.

Techniques: **A+**(100-95), A (94-90), A- (89-85), B+ (84-80), B (79-75), B- (74-70), C (69 – below)

Skills	Remarks
1. Turning On the System.	
2. Closing the Open programs (e.g Ms Word).	
3. Clicking the start button and choosing Turn Off Computer.	
4. Clicking the Turn off button to turn off the computer.	
5. Arrange the chair and put the keyboard nicely.	

Quick-Check (16)

> **Fill in each blank with the correct answer from the brackets below.**

{
Food	clean	shoes	system
switch	UPS	door	Power
}

1.) Remove your _____ before you enter your computer room.

2.) Never take any _____ like toffees, chocolates, Chewing gum inside the computer room.

3.) Keep the computer room_____.

4.) Shut the _____ of the computer-room properly.

5.)   Turn on the switch at the source of the
                _____ SUPPLY.

6.)   Turn on the _____ to regulate the
       flow of current.

7.)   Turn on the POWER _____ of the
       Monitor.

8.)   Turn on the _____ UNIT.

My Scanner

Lesson – 7.1: WHAT IS A SCANNER?

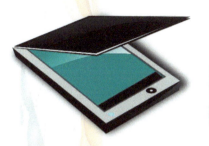

A multifunctional printer also has a scanner that helps it to get pictures from the printer.

♣ A scanner is used to copy pictures, document and others into the computer.

A scanner is a device that lets you copy images into the computer.

You can also photocopy the pictures or crop the picture to make them smaller.

Lesson – 7.2: TYPES OF SCANNER

There are many types of scanners, some basic types of scanners are mentioned below:

1. **Flatbed Scanner**

It copies an images into memory.

It is mostly use at the office, cyber café shop and home.

2. **Portable Scanner**

It copies an image by sliding across the image, making direct contact.

They are small and lightweight. Easy to carry.

 3. Optical Scanner

Teachers, students and lawyers use optical scanner to record information. It is used to copy document into a file for future use.

 4. Barcode Scanner

Super-market and Book-store use barcode scanner to read bar code on a product.

Quick-Check (17)

Draw a line to match each picture with the correct information.

Super-market and Bookshop

Teachers, Students and lawyers

small and lightweight. Easy to carry

Offices, cyber café shop and home.

Chapter - 8

My Modem

Lesson – 8.1: What is a modem?

♣ Modem is a computer device used to send and receive digital information between computers.

Lesson – 8.2: TYPES OF MODEM

1.) **Cable modem**.

It uses a cable to send and receive digital information.

2.) **Wireless modem**.

It does not need a cable to transfer or receive information.

3.) **USB modem or Mobile Partner**.

It must be inserted into a laptop or a desktop computer using USB port.

PUZZLE GAME ON PARTS OF THE COMPUTER

➢ Nine parts of a Desktop computer are hidden in the puzzle.

➢ The words may go across, down or diagonally. Use the words given below to help you.

➢ One example has been given to you.

Monitor	Mouse	Modem
Microphone	Keyboard	Printer
~~System unit~~	Scanner	Speaker

INSTRUCTION: You have to trace the answers both **verticals (↓)** and **horizontals (→).**

G	A	M	E	Z	P	O	R	T	E	L	E	V	I	S	I	O	N
A	E	H	H	A	S	N	A	K	E	M	O	U	T	H	M	O	V
L	R	O	A	B	S	Y	S	T	E	M	A	U	N	I	T	S	A
O	O	U	N	Y	P	H	O	T	S	O	H	O	P	S	S	T	O
O	P	S	D	S	E	H	E	L	L	D	W	E	L	C	O	M	E
N	L	E	P	T	A	F	A	N	D	E	L	E	P	H	A	N	T
R	A	R	H	M	K	E	Y	B	O	A	R	D	P	R	I	M	A
O	N	O	O	N	E	H	U	M	I	L	I	A	T	I	O	N	Y
A	E	O	N	Q	R	Q	E	E	N	O	F	M	O	T	H	E	S
D	T	M	E	R	E	N	G	L	A	N	D	O	R	A	N	G	C
S	M	K	U	C	U	M	B	E	R	P	U	N	I	C	E	F	A
M	O	D	E	M	O	N	K	E	Y	R	C	I	N	C	H	E	N
O	N	A	P	O	L	E	A	N	D	O	K	T	E	L	L	S	N
U	N	I	G	T	Y	G	N	A	L	G	S	O	L	D	O	D	E
S	E	R	I	A	L	H	G	E	S	R	P	R	I	N	T	E	R
E	O	I	L	R	T	S	A	R	O	E	O	I	O	R	E	D	I
S	H	I	R	T	E	H	R	E	T	S	R	N	N	B	R	O	W
S	K	I	R	T	O	H	O	F	N	S	T	T	Y	E	L	L	O
T	O	U	S	E	R	S	O	B	W	P	A	E	B	L	U	E	D
F	L	A	S	H	D	M	I	C	R	O	E	P	H	O	N	E	O

Quick-Check (18)

Tick the correct answer

$\overline{3}$

1. A modem which has no wire that connects it to the computer is called ………………………... (   )

    (a.) Wireless Modem
    (b.) Traditional Modem
    (c.) Mobile Partner

2. A modem which has a wire that connects it to the computer is called ……………………... (   )

    (a.) Wireless Modem

(b.) Mobile Partner

(c.) Traditional Modem

3. Which picture shows a modem?   (   )

(a.)

(c.)

(b.)

Test

14

SECTION-A
Draw lines to connect the parts of the computer to their name.

Monitor

Mouse

Microphon

System

Speaker

Scanner

Keyboard

Printer

SECTION-B

18

Name three types of the computer mouse using the names below.

(**Traditional**,   **Optical**,   **Optical wireless**)

1. _____ mouse has no trackball, but have long cable and a sensor.

2. _____ mouse has no trackball and no long-cable, but it has a USB-connector and a sensor.

3. _____ mouse has a trackball and a long-cable.

Circle the correct answer from the given options.

4. I look like a table tennis ball, who am I? _____.
   a. Trackball   b. Long-cable   c. Buttons

5. I look like a rope, who am I? _____.
   a. USB-Connector   b. Trackball   c. Long-cable

6. I am used to rest the palm, who am I? _____.
   a. Trackball   b. Palm-rest   c. Buttons

7. I look like a memory stick, who am I? _____.
   a. Trackball   b. USB-Connector   c. Scroll-
                                                               wheel

8. I am used to click and double-click, who am I? _____.
   a. Buttons   b. USB-Connector   c. Long-cable

9. The mouse is used to _____ or _____ on your
   screen.
   a. point, click   b. point, dance   c. point, sleep

INTRODUCTION TO COMPUTER-1 (Starter)

18

INSTRUCTION:

Find the missing letter in each part of the computer. No.1 has been done for you.

1. Com **p** uter

2. Mon__tor

3. __ouse

4. K__yboard

5. S__anner

6. Printe__

INTRODUCTION TO COMPUTER-1 (Starter)

7. Spe__ker

8. Syste__ Un__t

9. Mi__rophone

10. Tele__ision

INTRODUCTION TO COMPUTER-1 (Starter)

References:

- Alan Simpson, What is Hardware? [Online], Available: http://www.coolnerds.com/newbies/hardware/hardware.htm [Accessed 10 February 2010]

- (No Name)(19 December 2010) What are computers? [Online]. Available: http://wikieducator.org/User:Tzaynah/TComputingCourse [Accessed 10 August 2010]

- Jeff Dunn, (*November 2, 2013*) 10 Important Rules For Your School's Computer Lab , Nov. 2, 2013[Online], Available: http://www.edudemic.com/school-computer-lab-rules [Accessed 21 January 2014]

- Vic Laurie, Mouse exercises [Online]. Available: http://www.seniornet.org/howto/mouseexercises/mousepractice.html [Accessed 10 August 2010]

- (No Name) (Feb 22, 2013), Learn Parts Of The Body [Online]. Available: https://www.youtube.com/watch?v=mmt-IF_3Bzw [Accessed 21 January 2014]

- Slide Share, (*Feb 24, 2008*) Printers and Scanner [Online]. Available: http://www.slideshare.net/askme/chapter-11-280487 [Accessed 1 June 2016]

- Free High Quality Images [Online]. Available: https://pixabay.com/ [Accessed 14 June 2016]